50⁰⁰

# STAIRCASES

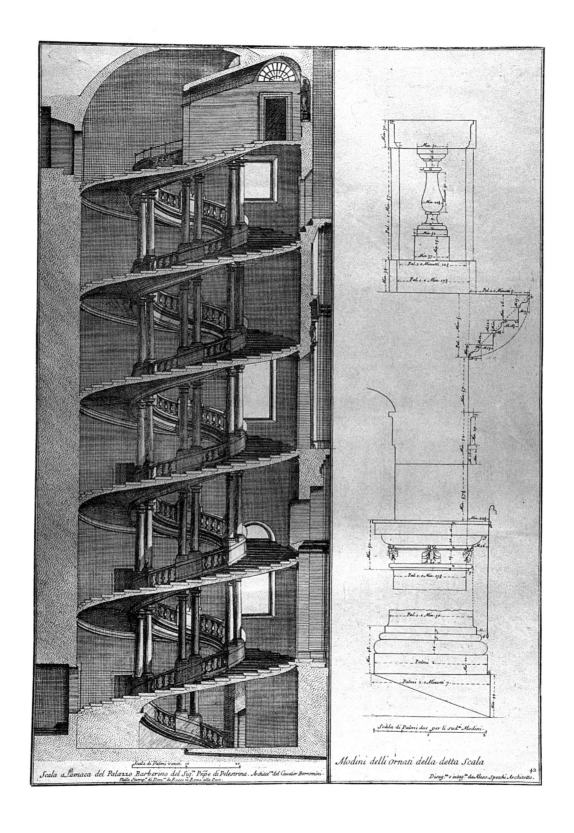

Scala di Palmi venti.

Scala a Lumaca del Palazzo Barberino del Sig.re Prîpe di Pelestrina. Architet.to del Cavalier Borromini.
Nella Stamp.a di Dom.co de Rossi in Roma alla Pace.

Modini delli Ornati della detta Scala.

Scala di Palmi due, per li sud.ti Modini.

Diseg.to e intag.to da Aless. Specchi Architetto.

42

# STAIRCASES

MICHAEL SPENS

## DETAIL IN BUILDING

ACADEMY EDITIONS

# DETAIL IN BUILDING

Advisory Panel: Maritz Vandenberg, Christopher Dean, Christopher McCarthy, Michael Spens

*ACKNOWLEDGEMENTS*

Attempts have been made to locate sources of all photographs to obtain full reproduction rights, but in the very few instances where this process has failed to find the copyright holder, apologies are offered. Photographic credits: Richard Bryant/Arcaid, pp20-21; Scott Frances/Esto Photographics, pp26, 29; Jo Reid and John Peck, pp22, 23 (centre); Christian Richters, pp46, 48; Kim Zwarts, p54. Grateful acknowledgement is due to Penguin Books for permission to reproduce the following illustrations from Nikolaus Pevsner, *An Outline of European Architecture*, London, 1960: pp8 (right), 9, 12 (right), 15 (centre right). Several images in this book have been previously published elsewhere, and the author would like to thank those who have made it possible to reproduce them here: p8 (left and centre) from the facsimilie edition *I Quattro Libri dell'Architettura di Andrea Palladio*, Venice, 1570, published by Hoepli, Milan, 1918; pp10 (left), 15 courtesy of Giulio Roisecco (*L'Architettura del Ferro, l'Inghilterra 1688-1914*) and the publisher Bulzoni, Rome, 1972; pp11 (left), 16, 17 (below left) courtesy of Michael Spens; p11 (right) courtesy of A & C Black, publishers of *British Buildings 1960-69*, Stephen, Frampton and Carpetian, photograph by M Carpetian; p12 (left) courtesy of James Stirling, Michael Wilford and Partners, photograph by Timothy Hursley, Arkansas office; p12 (centre) courtesy of Giulio Roisecco and Bulzoni, Rome, 1969; p13 (above left and centre left) from *Otto Wagner* by Heinz Geretzegger and Max Peitner, Pall Mall Press, London, 1970; p13 (above right) reproduced as a detail from the original painting, courtesy of the Trustees of the National Gallery, London, with acknowledgement to Sir Ernst Gombrich; pp13 (centre right), 22 (above right) John Allan, RIBA Publications and the Executry of Berthold Lubetkin; pp13 (below left), 14 (left) courtesy of Richard Rogers and Partners, Architects; p13 (below right) courtesy of Herbert Felton; p14 (right) from *The Complete Works of Robert and James Adam* by Dr David King, Butterworth-Heinemann, Oxford, 1991, photograph by A Kersting; p17 (above right) photograph by the late Rob Hunter; p17 (centre) courtesy Max Dupain, Melbourne; p17 (below right) Juhani Pallasmaa and Patrick Degommier, Museum of Finnish Architecture. Caption and sketches on p23 are by Nicholas Grimshaw, courtesy of Ernst & Sohn publishers. The author would also like to thank Cristina Fontoura and Sara Parkin for their help in producing this book.

*Cover:* Jestico & Whiles, British Council Offices, Madrid, internal staircase
*Page 2:* Spiral staircase designed by Francesco Borromini (1599-1667) for the Palazzo Barberini, Rome

First published in Great Britain in 1995 by
ACADEMY EDITIONS
An imprint of

ACADEMY GROUP LTD
42 Leinster Gardens, London W2 3AN
Member of the VCH Publishing Group

ISBN 1 85490 416 7

Distributed to the trade in the United States of America by
NATIONAL BOOK NETWORK, INC
4720 Boston Way, Lanham, Maryland 20706

Printed and bound in Great Britain

# CONTENTS

# INTRODUCTION

Throughout the twentieth century, the stair as an element of architecture has maintained the importance which has been attributed to it since the Renaissance. Such a status still derives from a combination of utility, or functional considerations, with an inherent aesthetic potential in terms of both the articulation of the structural form, and its further enhancement. The status of staircases might have been expected to diminish markedly with the advent of the elevator or lift in the nineteenth century. Perhaps surprisingly, this has not been the case. Notwithstanding the result of this advance – whereby all circulation requirements of routine passage, whether commercial or residential, could be supplied in this effortless manner (at least for reaching any level over three floors) – the staircase has remained a major element in the building design, plan and section. Basic statutory fire escape provision has of course ensured that the staircase legally remains an essential means of escape in emergency, and as a stand-by circulation in the event of mechanical failure or power interruption; hence the combination of circumstances that paradoxically ensure that the staircase remains a primary element in architectural design.

# DEFINITION

The stair is defined as 'an ascending series' or 'flight' of steps leading from one level to another, especially from one floor to another, as in a house – a staircase. The word itself derives from Old Teutonic *staigri*, and the terms stairway and staircase have come to be the established usage for the collective element, incorporating the steps, supporting framework, banisters, balusters and handrail. The element as such is therefore 'the staircase', abbreviated in common usage to 'the stairs' or 'stair'.

# HISTORY

The stair was evident in the architecture of prehistory, as at Knossos in Crete, (1600-1400 BC) but in a succession of civilisations was seen to remain an essentially static, monolithic arrangement of steps. Even the Roman talent for civil engineering contributed little to the advancement of the stair, other than to take advantage of the load-bearing economy of the arch. The section of the Colosseum AD 72-80 demonstrates this technique, where marble steps on the first and second levels (contiguous with the seating) give way to timber tiers and steps above.

As late as the medieval period (1000-1450) the stair seemed to be cast in the role of awkward accessory. Nonetheless, it was elementary to the movement between floors, most significantly from ground-level entrance to first-floor hall or *piano nobile*. An early decision in construction had to be made by master masons and their patrons, for example, as to whether to provide low step-heights (ie 'risers') to allow armour-clad knights to move easily up or down stairs, or whether to increase the dimension of the step vertically to give defenders above a positive advantage over attackers below them. Such were matters of life and death rather than of convenience pure and simple. The late medieval staircase at the château of Blois, and the double-newel stair at Chambord (where the same stairwell incorporated twin-parallel spirals), developed over the years 1515-25, signalled a new period of expression for the staircase. It is evident however, from contemporary documentation, that such an advance in technique required no less than the mature talent of Leonardo da Vinci himself, who died at nearby Amboise in 1519, the year work began at Chambord. Stair sketches by Da Vinci give clear evidence of not only double, but also quadruple solutions.

In the villa architecture of the sixteenth century, as exemplified by schematic plans of eleven of Palladio's own villas, it is significant that the staircase was still effectively marginalised, well after Da Vinci's death. What is also important is the

 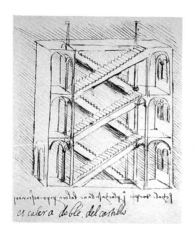 

reality of the staircase remaining a key punctuating item in the game of formal articulation, albeit within the building envelope, and the positioning of the stair or twin stairs remains fundamental. In other words, as a visual element the stair is muted, yet its essential presence in the plan form cannot be denied in the same way.

At the Escorial palace in Spain (1563-84) an Imperial Staircase (as it was to be known) was constructed under the influence of Da Vinci sketches. Here, an oblong space is first penetrated by a straight single run to a landing, at which a 180-degree turn gives access to an upper level by means now of two separate parallel runs, one to the left and one to the right.

In the mid-seventeenth century, Borromini's design for a spiral stair within the Palazzo Barberini in Rome created a masterpiece of elegant spatial definition of vertical ascent with the minimum of interval. Bernini's Scala Regia (1663-66) is its linear equivalent, the principal ceremonial route gives entry to the Vatican Palace, allowing the maximum processional advantage to scenic effect.

In Vienna in the early eighteenth century, Lukas von Hildebrandt (1668-1745) had brought a new baroque spatial emphasis to bear upon the staircase, in the Upper Belvedere; and it was in Germany, soon after, that Balthasar Neumann (1687-1753) made the staircase a central feature in his composition for the palaces at both Wurzburg and at Bruchsal. This development came as a natural progression via Hildebrandt's baroque church architecture. Increasingly, the staircase occupied a central role in the expression of spatial form in great public buildings in Europe. Alberti's earlier dictum, that the fewer staircases there are in a building and the less space they take up the better, was now wholly obsolete.

Such centrality for the staircase now seems a natural characteristic of the grandeur of the imperial architectures of the eighteenth and nineteenth-century

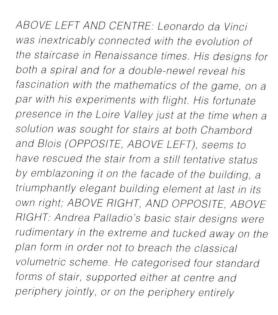

*ABOVE LEFT AND CENTRE: Leonardo da Vinci was inextricably connected with the evolution of the staircase in Renaissance times. His designs for both a spiral and for a double-newel reveal his fascination with the mathematics of the game, on a par with his experiments with flight. His fortunate presence in the Loire Valley just at the time when a solution was sought for stairs at both Chambord and Blois (OPPOSITE, ABOVE LEFT), seems to have rescued the stair from a still tentative status by emblazoning it on the facade of the building, a triumphantly elegant building element at last in its own right; ABOVE RIGHT, AND OPPOSITE, ABOVE RIGHT: Andrea Palladio's basic stair designs were rudimentary in the extreme and tucked away on the plan form in order not to breach the classical volumetric scheme. He categorised four standard forms of stair, supported either at centre and periphery jointly, or on the periphery entirely*

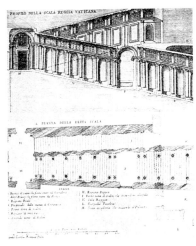

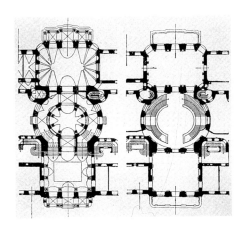

*CENTRE LEFT: Bramante's spiral stairway in the Belvedere Court at the Vatican (c 1503) appears to dispense with steps, becoming effectively a spiral ramp. The masonry and columnar structure is robust in the extreme, denoting the extreme caution arising from the prevalent technology; CENTRE RIGHT: Scala Regia, the Vatican. Fontana's drawing in plan and section makes clear the extent to which a grand staircase can, even exaggeratedly, emphasise the drama inherent in processional use, even to the extent of establishing a false perspective to this end; BELOW: Balthasar Neumann's staircase at Bruchsal in Germany, brought the stair to still greater heights of elegant beauty. The plan shows how it sweeps up an oval space in stages, with seemingly effortless grace. The external wall of the staircase is solid, while the inner wall creates Piranesian views down to an oval grotto. Conversely, moving upwards, the spatial sensation lightens increasingly until a form of plateau is reached, of the same oval area as the space enclosed below, and flooded with light. From here, there are views of a superb stuccoed cartouche in the dome overhead. Here is the staircase as an end in itself, its own aesthetic fulfilment per se*

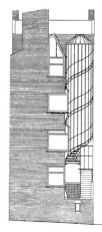

European powers, with the need for rhetoric, procession and display by those in power. That it persisted into the twentieth century, extended into the major civic buildings of both East and West, comes as no surprise. But these gestures denied the technical inventiveness that now established both lift/elevator and escalator as an effortless and potentially dramatic and superior means of ascent.

With the development of the Modern Movement in the 1920s, Alberti's postulation could have taken new effect with a vengeance. The proliferation of rapid vertical means of mechanical ascent within high buildings might have meant that Alberti's dictum would have proved logically correct. It says something fundamental about the sensibilities of architects and their clients that the stair, this 'difficult' test for first year students of building, made for a positive challenge for further development as an architectural element. Logically, it could have been relegated to the status of discreet accessory.

In the development of the new architecture of the first machine age (to use the term coined by P Reyner Banham) the articulation of the stair became increasingly refined and ever more sophisticated in detail. From the initial acceptance and display of spiral stairways by the early pioneers of rationalism, to the progression of grand internal access stairs demanded by public buildings for the new society, rationalism was obliged to broaden its own criteria to recognise that in major spaces, ceremony establishes its own functional brief.

From the domestic interior to the multi-storey exterior, the stair took on a new lease of life. A *raison d'être* spread from the 1920s which enabled a new definition of space to occur in the context of the staircase. Space, height, density and linkage with adjacent areas, all became factors in an intelligent game of architecture. In 1928 László Moholy-Nagy used a photograph he had taken of the air ventilation shaft of a ship to demonstrate the spatial propensities of the staircase, in vertical

*FROM L TO R: P Ellis, Jnr is famous for the cast-iron and plate glass 16 Cook Street (Liverpool, 1864-68) subsequently recognised by Louis Sullivan as a masterpiece of early cast-iron technology. H Russell Hitchcock discovered Ellis' building, with its highly sophisticated cast-iron spiral stair at the rear*

movement through air. Mart Stam's design for the stair shafts of the Van Nelle factory, Rotterdam (1927) demonstrated the essential role given to this element in the overall configuration of the building. In Alvar Aalto's Villa Mairea (1936) the stair is internal, yet entirely pivotal to the expression of the main entry space of the building. As Sigfried Giedeon said, 'it is often the manner in which the staircase is integrated into the spatial organisation of a house that betrays the architect's capacity for handling space'. At Mairea, the lightweight wooden staircase is allowed to flow softly into the main space, indicating the adjoining areas, yet maintaining its own autonomy, like a piece of transparent sculpture. At the Viipuri Library (completed in 1935) Aalto had used the vertical circulation to draw together the separate reading and lending areas, granting them a flowing quality, thus allowing the two areas to be readily supervised by one librarian. The main entrance was also articulated externally by a staircase enclosed in a single glass wall. In the brick-built MIT student dormitory building, the Baker House, Aalto again made the stairs the principal regulating element, expressed as such on the brick elevations, and so immediately revealing from outside the organising principle itself. At Cambridge, England, Leslie Martin, Colin St John Wilson and Patrick Hodgkinson used a similarly expressive stair elevation in the Caius College West Road hostel to revive the college staircase as a continuing symbol of the collegiate system of grouped accommodation.

As the post-war years receded in Europe, the United States and Japan, the divisions which naturally arose between differing schools of thought within the architectural community over the renewal or supercession of modernism, seemed only to unite on one point; of the importance of the stair. The stair as an element demanded the due expression of the capacity and significance it was granted in both public and private buildings alike. The high priests of Post-modernism

*FROM L TO R: Alvar Aalto, Baker House, Cambridge (Massachusetts, 1948) which demonstrated that the staircase can be a key generator when it fulfils a primary role in the planning of buildings for large numbers of students. In the 1990s, current students surveyed in the Aalto building still adjudged it a successful habitat; the staircase as a communal linking element is well utilised in the Caius College Hostel at West Road, Cambridge, and duly expressed elegantly on the external facade of this remarkable building by Martin, Wilson and Hodgkinson. Aalto's Baker House was clearly a precedent for this 1961 masterpiece*

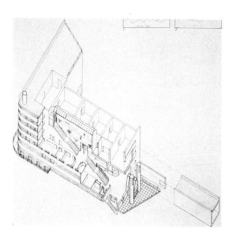

have generally praised Robert Venturi's grand staircase in the National Gallery in London (1985). Single flight staircases enhanced both Arata Isozaki's Art Gallery at Gumma in Japan and James Stirling's extension to the Fogg Museum at Harvard. In the ambulatories and great circulation lobbies of Hans Scharoun's Berlin Philharmonie, the stairway is the key to great architecture in the interplay of one level perambulatory space with another. In the British Library's main entrance hall (completion 1996) Colin St John Wilson's grand stairway succeeds in conveying both the utility and the poetics of spatial progression.

In Australia, Glenn Murcutt has reduced the contemporary stair to its minimalist extreme, in the Marsh and Freedman offices, Woolloomooloo, on two levels alone, in metal; and in timber to the same perfected degree, in the Carruthers Farm House at Mount Irvine (1978-80). In London, Nicholas Grimshaw & Partners have incorporated a superb staircase connecting three floors as a daily usable reminder of their continuing design principles. If that represents the state of the art in the 1990s internally, Will Alsop's external staircase below the Government Chamber in the Regional Headquarters building for Les Bouches du Rhône is the epitome of its external counterpart.

In the twenty-first century the staircase will, on current experience, remain a key element in the design iconography which architects continue to extend. Functional necessities have not reduced it to that marginal status which Alberti predicted at the birth of the Renaissance; logic could be said to have been confounded. Certainly, automatic methods of vertical circulation will develop new poetics themselves, but the staircase now remains embedded in the specification of buildings. Perhaps it is simply valid to forecast that as long as human aspirations predicate building requirements, there will always be a place for the stair.

In deeper focus there are timeless models. Otto Wagner's small stair designed

*FROM L TO R: James Stirling and Michael Wilford, extension to the Fogg Museum (Harvard, 1985) axonometric; Hans Scharoun exploits the sculptural expressionism of the staircase in the perambulatory spaces of the Philharmonie (Berlin, 1963) turning means of access and escape into a social function for movement for visitors during performance intervals; Walter Gropius and Adolf Meyer marked the emergence of early signs of modernism by designing transparent, equal and symmetrically disposed stair towers in an essentially classical plan and elevation. The solidity of the entrance elevation is in total contrast to the airy swirl of the twin staircase encased in steel and glass, Werkbund Exhibition Factory (Cologne, 1914)*

# NICHOLAS GRIMSHAW & PARTNERS

## OFFICES OF NICHOLAS GRIMSHAW & PARTNERS LTD, LONDON

*Internal Stair, 1992*

*I have always seen the office as part workshop and part studio. My ideal is for each team to have a working model beside them so that they can be continuously aware of the scale and size of the spaces on which they are working. Pieces are added and removed so that in the end the model has the feeling of a battered tapestry. One can also see pieces of buildings, castings and fixings lying around people's desks. This illustrates our constant dialogue with all the various manufacturers and suppliers. I enjoy showing the staircase to potential clients. I think they can appreciate the care that has gone into it. I hope they feel that if they appoint us as their architects they, too, will get the same degree of care and attention.*
Nick Grimshaw

When Nicholas Grimshaw & Partners converted a former 1920s factory in central London, the building was opened up both sideways and vertically, and a steel frame was inserted to replace the load-bearing original walls. Between the new extension and the original building, a top-lit stairway was inserted. This new central stair allows the office members and visitors ready access to every level. The stair which openly penetrates every level is mainly aluminium, so maintaining a lightweight loading and easy erection in such a constricted original space. Symbolically, the stair was assembled by hand and manoeuvred into place by Grimshaw and his staff; there was no on-site welding or drilling. The strings of the stairs are derived from available mast-sections (from the boat industry) and the treader (step) supports are inserted into the sail grooves on these masts. At either end of each flight, purpose-designed castings give bearings for the masts. Cast 'legs' offer fixing positions for tie rods. The treads with supports are standard aluminium sections, the tie rods are stainless steel. The combination of these elements (strings and legs) forms truss systems which reinforce the exceptionally lightweight structure. The handrails are continuously radiused tubular aluminium sections. Eventually, the two flights that exist will be extended upwards by a third, as easily as the first two were inserted.

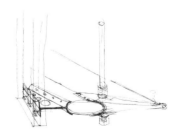

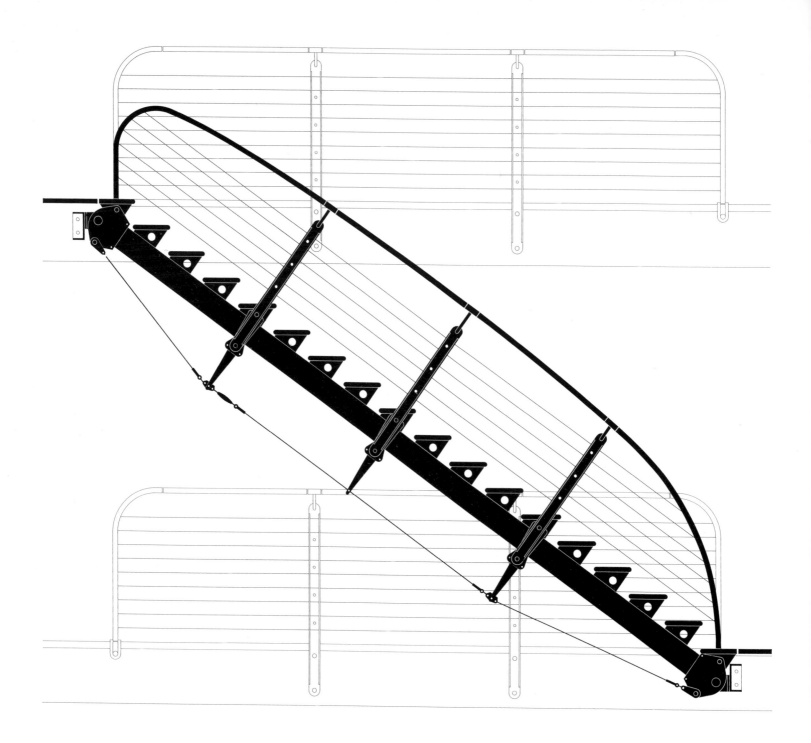

*Elevation*

# RICHARD MEIER ARCHITECTS

## HYPOLUX BANK, LUXEMBURG

*Internal Spiral Stair, 1993*

The Hypolux Bank building is itself a cylindrical volume, linked to an office slab, L-shaped in plan, upon a podium raised higher than adjacent street level. The spiral stair is located within the offices, in view of the cylindrical block outside. This cylinder houses the main reception areas and proclaims the presence of the bank, at both a local and a regional scale. The stair echoes the same form, itself spiralling within a regular cylindrical plan and volume. The curved monolithic skin of the stair itself rises within a cylindrical 'cage' which emphasises such characteristics and links three floors within the office slab.

A planted formal court with an ornamental pool serves to both define the surface of the podium and reflect the cylindrical screen wall containing the main entrance. Pedestrian access to this entry is via a short ramp, bridging the water and rising from the court to the entry floor suspended above the pool.

The L-shaped slab running parallel to the rue Alphonse Weicker is occupied by modular offices for most of its length. The southeastern end of this slab, adjacent to the cylinder, is given over on all four floors to semi-public bank functions which form an open atrium, while the opposite end is allocated to rental space with its own entrance. The offices have been carefully planned so as to provide a high degree of flexibility and efficiency while affording a certain individualism to each space through a syncopated window pattern.

The circular flow of the freestanding staircase contrasts with the rectilinear geometry of the offices slab and links across visually to the adjoining cylindrical bank block. Here the staircase fulfils a well-rehearsed articulation of vertical movement that contrasts with the flat geometry of the container which surrounds it. The parapet of the stair is repeated on the inside spiral, identical to the exterior, thus emphasising the spiral effect.

27

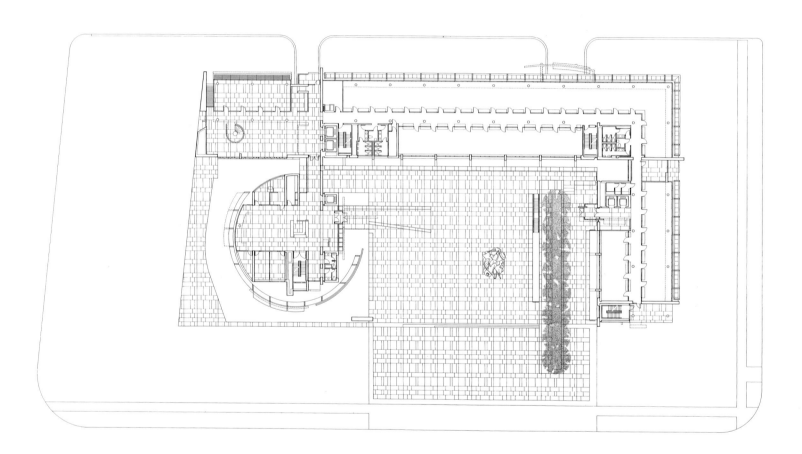

*Ground level plan*

# ALSOP & STÖRMER

## DÉLIBERATIF, LES BOUCHES DU RHÔNE, MARSEILLES

*External Staircase, 1994*

The single flight staircase descends from the Déliberatif – the chamber of government and symbolic centre of the whole complex – to ground level, creating an alternative form of grand entrance way to the building, and giving access to the extensive, sun-screened terrace on the east side of the chamber, where a soft canopy protects users of the stair. The stair fulfils an essential role in fire or security emergency by allowing, as a result of generous width, a rapid evacuation of the chamber and its ancillary offices. The structure consists of two Warren-type trusses made from hollow steel sections, whose bottom booms are restrained by the steps themselves and their supporting members, whereas the top booms are restrained by cross members. The resulting box structure is supported independently on two inclined trussed steel pylons, anchored to the ground slab via pin connections; the static and dynamic forces of the structure are transferred to the foundations through the basement parking concrete frame.

The drawings indicate a strong but relatively lightweight steel structure, clearly differentiated by its support system of steel frame from the slender, curved framework of the Déliberatif. This degree of separate articulation is necessary since it also visually expresses the idea of public accessibility, which, even if constrained by security requirements, characterises the whole building complex, and was a primary aim of the client's brief. This concept is applied in varying ways throughout the building, but here on the most public aspect, the staircases as constructed undoubtedly convey the notion of accessibility in a readily identifiable manner. Painted the same blue as the major fabric of the building exterior, it is clear that they are not differentiated by Alsop, but instead form single elements of equal status and meaning, in relation to the complete apparatus, co-existing as important ingredients in the whole assemblage, not simply as separate functioning parts.

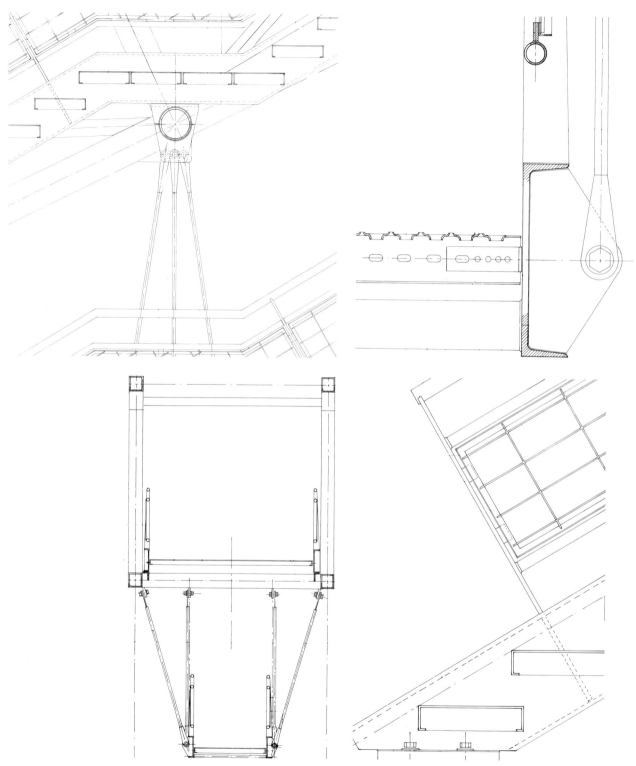

Details of staircase

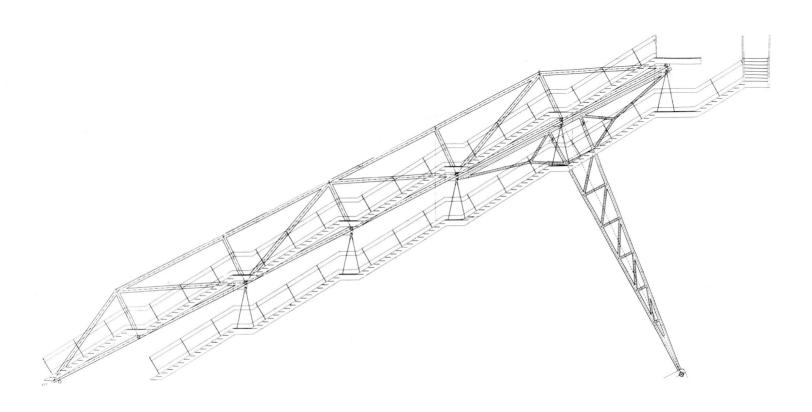

# ARKITEKTURBÜRO BOLLES-WILSON

## MUNSTER LIBRARY, GERMANY

*Internal Staircase, 1993*

This semi-circular library building holds its place in a distinguished line of libraries that have relied upon circular geometry to resolve the typological requirements imposed by the large-scale supervision and handling/transfer and storage of books. Bolles-Wilson have used a broken, incomplete drum-form that is duly embellished with four excellent stairs. From the lending section, a single flight of stairs leads dramatically to the main upper level. Voids of varying width emphasise this condition as they open onto the stairs. This flight incorporates intermediate 'landings' given the overall length of the run, an essential building regulation provision. The handrail emphasises this easement. On one side, where open, it is free-running, on the other side fixed to the wall. The treads are constructed from timber, and there are V-shaped, eight-metre-long supporting steel legs, which are only visible from the side of what is, in this case, the principal internal stair. The staircase as a whole fills a twenty-metre-high void. The steel structure is finished with a ferrous paint, and the beechwood treads retained their natural colour.

The staircase here described is one of a family of four purpose-designed stairs, where two are on the exterior of the building, in quite different situations, and two are internal. The two external stairs help to emphasise the organisational construction of the building in two blocks, which is emphatic in that it accepts a degree of fragmentation of role and use, and hence of formal layout in volume and plan. The two internal staircases engage simply with this orthogonal looseness, contributing to the opening-up process set up as a result. Bolles-Wilson are playing a highly sophisticated game that concedes historical reference to earlier iconic examples of Modernism: the staircase is used as an activated part, as befits a circulation element. Unlike, for example, the simple, linear access, street role fulfilled by the single flight stair designed at the Sackler Gallery for the Fogg Museum at Harvard (as employed by Sir James Stirling), Bolles-Wilson use the staircases internally both to provide an opening-up of spaces, but also to show the way forward, revealing the essence of the library spaces served and their relative importance to each other. The staircase shown, as one example from the four, is particularly effective in guiding the visitor/user arriving at the lending section on the second, upper level. Bolles-Wilson's use of 'running stairs' is invaluable in providing the visitor with immediate senses of direction, an aid usually woefully absent in such a building type. In the whole context, the role of Bolles-Wilson's staircases in this most articulate of library buildings is scarcely one of primary definition, rather it is one of subtle invitation and direction.

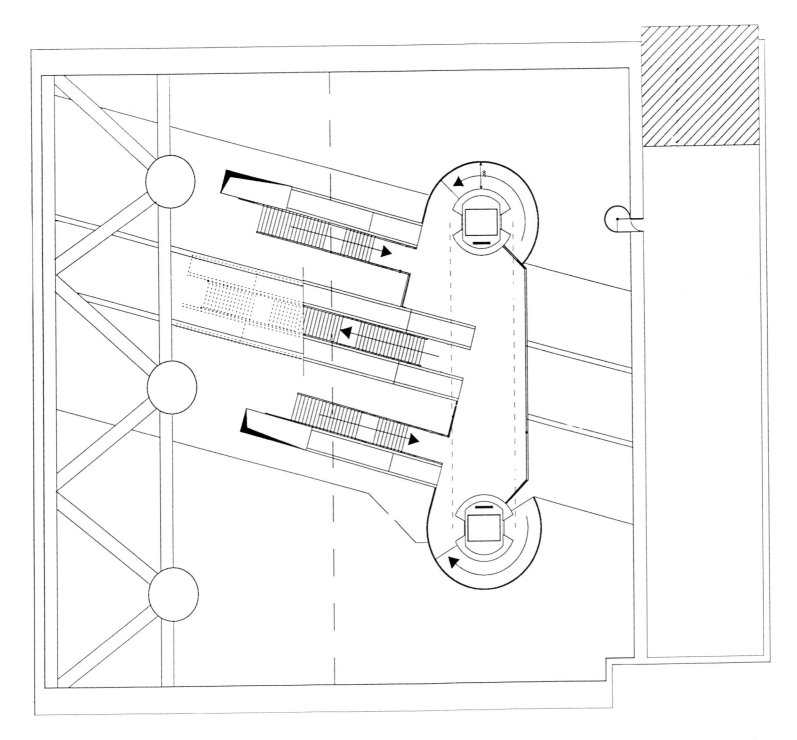

*Staircase plan*

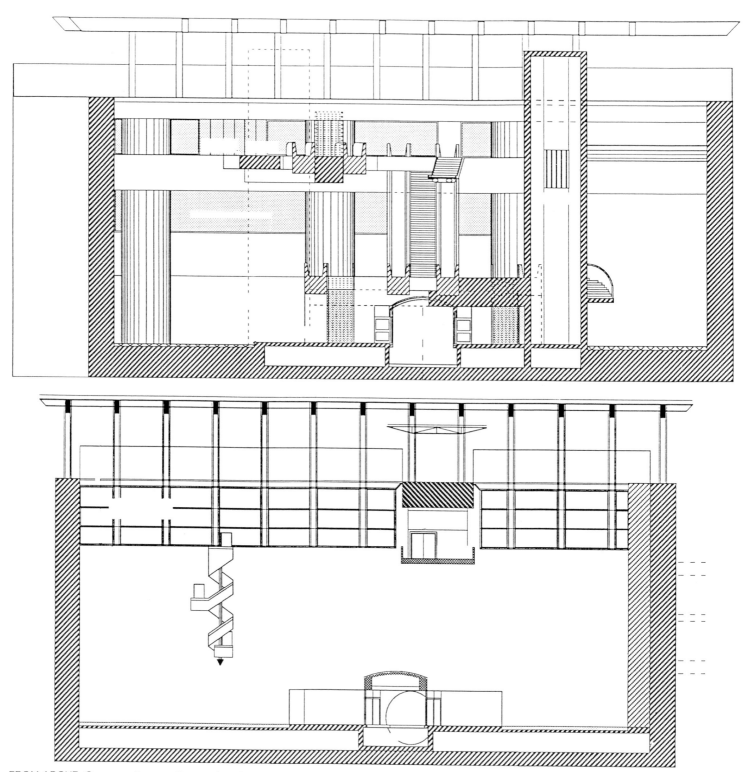

*FROM ABOVE: Cross section; southeast elevation*

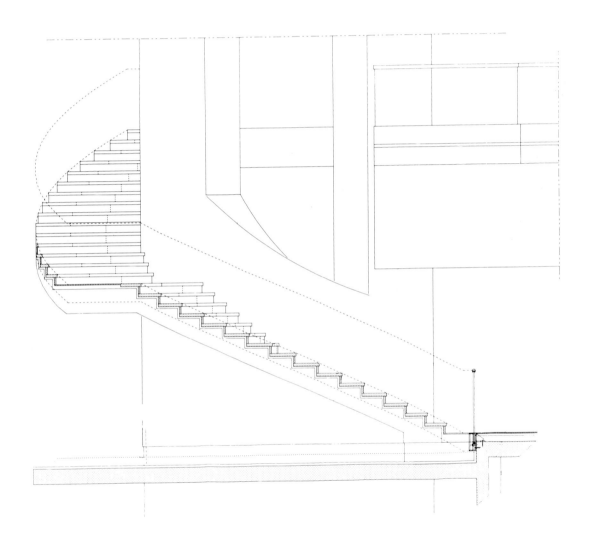

*Elevation*

59

# COLIN ST JOHN WILSON & PARTNERS

## BRITISH LIBRARY ENTRANCE, LONDON

*Grand Internal Staircase, 1995*

The move of the British Library from the British Museum to the new site next to St Pancras Station in Euston Road, has created a library of truly colossal scale. The main access stairway provided by Colin St John Wilson is approached following entry to the library from the main forecourt, which provides a degree of protection from one of London's busiest thoroughfares.

Wilson has established a space of great beauty, which at a glance allows the visitor to recognise the primary organisation of the building. Moving into the main body of the library, the visitor will have passed Sir Eduardo Paolozzi's statue of Isaac Newton, and it was intended that once inside the building the visitor would also see, adjacent to this grand stairway, a superb tapestry based on a painting by Ron Kitaj. The Portland stone stair itself is elementary in its simplicity, and the brass and leather-clad handrails with spiral binding (unfinished in the photograph) are intended, as in similar buildings by Alvar Aalto, whose influence Wilson admits, to permit a tactile and user-friendly condition, given the overall spatial monumentality of this great space. The stone treads of the stairs are neatly cut back and have PVC non-slip inserts. A combination of steel, leather and masonry relates well to the surrounding materials. Few architects today can rise to the challenge of working on this scale, and Wilson has achieved success with dexterity.

The grand staircase of the British Library emphasises the public face of a national institution. The building itself had been criticised by glib armchair exponents (one likened it to 'a training school for secret policemen') which revealed anxiety about the creation of such a massive contemporary space, and a lack of intimacy, even 'cosiness': suffice it to say that it is this very quality of openness that succeeds so richly. As befits a public resource (rather than a palace) this spatial quality enhances the ascent, at one level from the lobby leading off the entrance forecourt, linking upwards to the user levels (past a core historical library, a symbolic visual presentation of bound antiquities sheathed in glass). The leather-bound handrail is entirely in keeping with such qualities as must be evident in great libraries. This openness and accessibility operates within a nave-like concourse of cathedral-like splendour, yet Piranesian dramatics have no place here. This is a public space of a standard wholly unsurpassed in late twentieth-century Britain.

61

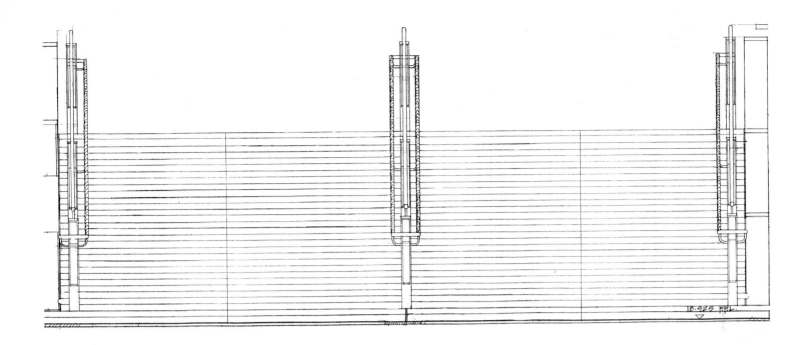

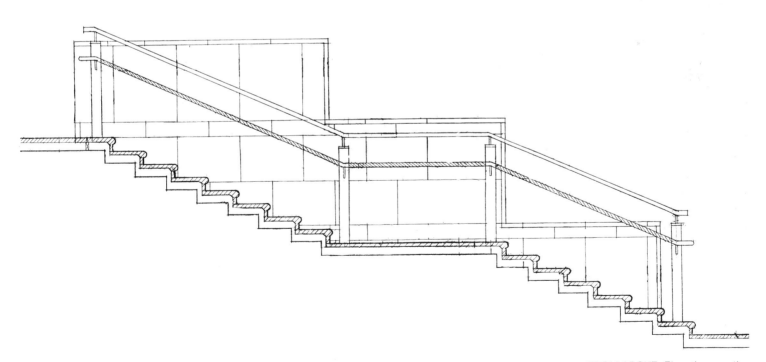

*FROM ABOVE: Elevation; section*

# FURTHER READING

Alan Blanc, *Stairs, Steps and Ramps*, Butterworth-Heinemann, Oxford, 1995.
This is an exemplary and fully detailed study of these elements, and is the most definitive currently available. It describes the full range of technical options available to designers, together with an excellent range of examples.

Christine-Ruth Hansmann, *Treppen in der Arkitektur* (Stairs in Architecture), DVA, Stuttgart, 1993.